THREE THINGS YOU NEED TO MAKE $1000 MONTHLY

BASSEY JIMMY

DEDICATION

This book is dedicated to the Almighty God for His Grace that has overwhelmed me and leads me in putting this piece of work together.

CONTENTS

ACKNOWLEDGMENTS

I am grateful to my friend, Wisdom who has helped in contributing as well as proof reading of this book itself.

I feel a deep sense of gratitude to my precious wife, Esther, and our children, Dominion, Blessing, Rhema and Joy for their patience and support from conception of this book to its present form. You are a gift to me, and may your gift continue to make a way for you in the world.

INTRODUCTION

Today, many individuals believe you need two heads to make $1000 every month but it's not so. There are another set of people who think this can only be achieved by working extra hours into the night; but yet this too is not true. Another set of individuals is of the opinion that you need to have a ton of experience before you can make this kind of money; this also would I say is fallacy.

No one has ever made it right by assumptions and hear say. You only need a determination, a working platform and a proven strategy to make $1000 monthly.

This book is written to explain to you the steps you need to make $1000 monthly. This is doable if you follow this book judiciously and apply all the steps explicitly explained.

Take your time to read through this book maybe thrice or more until you have fully understood the concept of making $1000 monthly.

Making money is fun when you know what you're doing especially when you have a hungry audience who need your services.

1 CHAPTER ONE

Everything starts with Determination

Most people struggle to stay motivated due to negative thoughts and anxiety about the future. Even though every man faces depression and doubt, the ability to move forward is what makes one successful.

Therefore, determination is the key to success. Determination is pursuing your goals against all odds until manifestation. It is working assiduously to get desirable results no matter the obstacles and challenges. When your mind is filled up with positive thoughts and your aim is fully on the task ahead, you are on the path of achievements. If you do this persistently and continuously, you can pull yourself out of any setback.

To be determined, you must be self motivated and have a strong internal drive for success. Your determination must be characterized with resilience if your set short-term or long-term goals must be achieved.

3 Keys That Boost Determination

Confidence

There is nothing that kills determination like lack of confidence. This comes to play when you target a goal, and while still on it, your mind begins to present explanations for why you aren't meeting the goal. This in turn creates thoughts that are negative. Your mind becomes filled up with thoughts of past failures, and personal weaknesses. Whenever you start giving excuses about your success and linking up with competitors, you create a bad impression about yourself and others, losing self confidence.

Gratitude is what you can use to change your thought pattern. Learn to focus all your attention on everything positive in life. List out what you are sure you can achieve and add to it others things you know can do in the nearest future. Never dwell on your past failures, look beyond the mistakes and blunders you made. Your continuous effort to be grateful can open a whole lot of opportunities, making you realize how prolific and successful you are. This is the only way you can boost your confidence and ride on it to your success.

You must learn to create value and be a solution to problems. Only then will you make money and be successful online.

Focus

The second key to determination is focus. It's focus that will take away fear and help you arrive at your set goals. To be successful online, set your focus on the things you need do to be successful. Avoid fear by all means because it can drain out all hope of being successful.

 If you're caught up thoughts that are based on fear, the first thing to do is to focus your energy on a well defined plan of achieving your goal. By having a set goal, you involuntarily define a set of measures of success. If you have a fear of failure, create a plan to succeed. It could be hiring a tutor, having a business partner, or saving for the future. The key is to move from an indefinable need to something tangible and lasting.

Focus your mind on something positive instead of dwelling on fear. Think, and create a way to succeed. Instead of worrying about tomorrow, start to do something about it today. This is the way to motivate you to take action. When know what you want, n matter the initial outcome, you are motivated to take action.

Direction

This is what put confidence and focus into play. Focus means having and setting an ultimate goal, while direction is to have a step by step strategy to achieve it. Lack of direction extinguishes determination because without achievable goals, we give in to procrastination. Don't spend hours writing articles when actually you should be busy putting up your affiliate sales page. This does not rhyme at all.

To find direction, you need to identify the activities that lead to success. For every goal you set to achieve, there are activities that bring results and others that can't. Create a list of all your activities and arrange them according to priority. Then take an action plan that dwells mainly on the activities yielding big returns. To continue the example from above, an affiliate's list would look something like this:

1. Select a profitable niche
2. Write contents and articles
3. Build a blog or website
4. Get traffic
5. Create an email list from your site's visitors
6. Promote your affiliate links to your site visitors
7. Optimize design and ad placements on your site
8. Answer comments and emails
9. Post on social media sites/forums
10. Rinse and repeat

Continue to keep track of your important tasks as it will direct your energy towards success. It's easy to waste your day entirely on minor activities like chatting on facebook, watching videos on Youtube if you are not disciplined.

Split your goals into short term and long term goals with the former dealing on small, while the latter should be a long-term goal. It is a fact that you will experience depression, failure and sometimes regret in the course of pursuing your goals. But if you can't discipline your mind, these minor issues can turn into great challenges. Embracing these three keys you can achieve whatsoever you want in life and be successful even in businesses online.

The power of a positive mindset

There is how you will enter in business that you will not encounter hard times, success, failure and also lots of ups and downs. The key to stay fit and resolute is to ignore what happens to you and choose to be better and better each day.

With a positive attitude, you are bound to exhibit a positive energy and drive which will connect customers to your business world. But if you decide to be clumsy because you had one negative event, you are bound to lose your existing customers and those who come in contact with you.

Attitude is infectious and will surely affect those who come around you. So be positive minded because everything is from the inside.

For you to succeed in online business and make $1000 monthly, a positive approach is needed by you to make you feel confident and in perfect control. When you are in perfect control, peak performance is inevitable.

Don't dwell on negative thoughts. Always think of right ways to make your plan work. Concentrate your attention on whatever you have to do in bringing your dreams to reality.

Remember that staying positive prevents damage to your confidence, mental skills and health.

Say no to your comfort zone

Your comfort zone can stop you from becoming and doing many things in life. To be successful and scale to greater heights in your life, you must be ready to face your fears and every other hindrance hindering the manifestation of your dreams.

Everything you've ever desire is one step outside your comfort zone. Comfort zone has killed ideas, opportunities, result oriented actions and growth in life and businesses than everything else in the world combined.

It's only outside your comfort zone that you learn new ideas, grow and develop beyond your wildest dreams. The only way worth living is to live uncomfortably; knowing this is not where you suppose to be and creating a road map which will help you locate your finished line.

To succeed and make $1000 monthly, you'll need to push yourself into new areas where you will have a chance to authentically define who you are, breaking out from limitations that hinder you.

You must stretch yourself to grow and discover things you couldn't have done and achieve were you still boxed up in your comfort zone. If you are open to challenges, take risk on issues bothering on finance and growth, you will break records and clear out every obstacles around your business.

When you take risk, you are ready to gamble with something you are willing to lose. These losses will then teach you something such as making your product better or how you can market differently and still get results.

Celebrate when you win and motivate yourself, and then move to the next line of action without delay.

Do away with Procrastination

To be successful in life, you must hate procrastination by all standards. I have come across individuals who spend days, weeks and months planning and staying "busy" without doing something tangible. They only propose to start a business which after months of waiting, they still are not ready to go ahead and start.

For you to make $1000 monthly, you must make up your mind to take your tasks, plans and goals seriously, doing what needed to be done without postponing anything to another date or time.

Tips on avoiding procrastination

1. Make a list

Many successful individuals uses list to keep procrastination away. The internet has so developed that there are tools you can easily use to create a list; daily planners, software etc.

2. Take short steps

Set priorities on your list. Start with smaller jobs that you can manage. These will keep away fear and kill any anxiety you might have had. With discipline and a clear vision, you can focus your thoughts and priorities on what really matters.

3. Forget Perfection for now

At the start, don't look out for perfection. Just start your business and as you continue to delve into it, you'll easily fine turn such and make it better.

4. Write down things consistently

Make it a daily routine to check your progress and the impact you have added to your business. For example, if you happen to make 3 sales in a week, think of ways of improving your strategy and getting up to seven or eight sales next week to come without breaking your goals.

5. Remember your dreams and stick to it

This is one of the key pointers to note. Let your initial dream be the drive you need when it is unbearable and you out of focus for things you might not be able to handle.

6. Ignore shiny objects you see everyday. Don't fall for quick-rich schemes. Follow up on your plans. Don't delay the steps required to fulfill your ambitions.

7. **Trying out new things** is a great way of occupying your mind and time.

Be ready to ride on obstacles

Every part of our lives is crowded by obstacles. There is no aspect of our lives namely career, business, marriage, family and relationships that we have not encountered an obstacle before.

It's worthy of note that there can not be any growth without obstacles. The best of any man is manifested when he is faced by an obstacle. To achieve your dreams you need to work hard and overcome all troubles and challenges you might encounter.

If you are determined to make $1000 monthly, you will be faced with stiff competitions, trials, network failures, error approach, getting out of timeline, difficulty in convincing a client to buy, unexpected requests for refund, people's opinion, bad results, failures and other unexpected obstacles, all out to frustrate your desired business goals.

Even though it may be tough and the cloud looks dark for you, be assured that these things are there to help you control your emotions, actions, and decisions empowering you to focus on achieving your business goals ultimately.

Tips to overcome obstacles in business

1. Be empowered in your mind that you can make come what may.

2. Have a concrete vision concerning your business and stick to it.

3. Know what you want and put your focus on achieving just that.

4. Don't settle for less, against all odds maintain your stand.

5. Do away with worry, anxiety and fear of failure as the three are the greatest obstacles to achieving anything in life.

6. Don't compare yourself with others. Compare yourself only to yourself and what you aspire to become.

7. Don't put blame on anybody or anything. Take responsibility for your failures and successes alike. Spend time fixing the problem instead of trading blame with others.

8. Don't be distracted by whatever. Starve yourself of distractions and feed only on focus.

2 CHAPTER TWO

The importance of information

The internet is a marketplace and for you to succeed, you need to follow the rules and principles that govern it. It is how you act and behave in the market that determines your results. You can waste your time online like others without achieving any thing or you can sit tight and make up your mind to do something for your life by focusing on an area to make money online. It is just a choice.

For you to get the best out of internet business, you need to arm yourself securely and press on without any fear of failure or distractions. The following are the tools you need to achieve your online business dream.

Develop a success mindset

First and foremost, you must think, see, believe and live success if you really want to make it online. It is a challenge to succeed and that challenge starts from the mind. If it wasn't, I am sure many people would have become successful. It took me months to finally succeed online after years of struggling. Success only came when I realized I had all it takes to make it online. I then knew I need to push and believe in myself I can do it no matter what I experienced.

In life you will discover that only a minute percent of the world population (about 3%) are really busy enjoying life and making it big. Why is it so? The answer boils down to the fact that only those few enjoying life is the ones who take time to plan and dream. And no matter the pains, struggles and challenges they had, the followed up their dream to reality.

Set up a plan and follow it up. Continue in it and refine your plans and you will definitely succeed. You have to see the future finished in advance. You have to put in long hours to achieve your dreams. You have got to put up with setbacks and disappointments.

Know that without discipline there is no success. It becomes imperative that in any business you do or strive to do, you must learn to enjoy the process of discipline and putting yourself through the process of discipline. You're your challenge squarely, forget about competition, and don't give in to your blunders. Learn from your mistakes and take steps to becoming the best. Then you will be successful.

So as you want to start, change your mindset, and believe you can and see yourself riding up to success.

Embrace knowledge and information

Every successful businessman seeks for knowledge and gathers information as if it is the end. Likewise, in online business don't let relevant business information and advice passes you. It is an error for you to believe you know too much. Information is never old. Information is the key to your breakthrough as it will aid you to know what is trending, what your competitors are doing and actions you need to take to beat them.

These things usually happen when you gather the right information in preparation to start an online business.

- Know what you want to do
- Know your targeted market
- Know how it is being done
- Create your niche
- Promote to your targeted clients/customers
- Learn the tricks to keep your clients/customers
- Discover ways of beating your competitors
- How to spend less funds in business setup
- Tools and techniques needed to expand and keep going.
- Give you firsthand information about others who had trailed the same path – their driving force, their strength and weaknesses.

I have discovered in my many years of online marketing that it is only through information that:

- You get to know how to get customers through the back door cost effectively.
- You define your own way of retaining the customers and how to keep them coming for more.

- Show you how to put together a money making strategy that customers will always value.

In addition to gathering of information and gaining knowledge, you need to learn new skills and discover your emotions. It is how we feel about what we know that makes the biggest difference in how our lives turn out to be. How you feel about the opportunities online you have and the choices you have determines the intensity of your effort to succeed.

So go ahead, develop yourself. Gather as much information as you can before you venture into any online business. Learn, practice, put passion into it and you will find yourself doing the unthinkable; breaking new grounds and making unending money online.

Places to gather information

Thanks to the internet, below are some of the different ways of gathering information for your online business.

- Google Search
- Blogs related to products and services
- Ebooks
- Videos
- Webinars
- Email marketing
- Articles Sites
- Social bookmarking sites
- Social media sites
- Forums

- Joint ventures
- Online training
- Webcast
- Podcast

Beware of Scam/Fraud

It is absolutely true that the internet is full of fraudsters and scammers. But since the internet is a powerful tool for business, you can't just avoid doing your business. This book is committed to letting you know how to know authentic business on the web and avoid being scammed.

You could lose nothing if you can detect fraud warning signals and avoid danger in carrying out your business deals online. You need to be smart, sensible and observant when dealing with people online

Signs of Fraud

With these simple ways which could easily be detected, you will definitely see fraud signals hanging in your face.

- When the business promises little or no risk at all.
- When a business offers to give you large returns on investments
- Catchy advertising
- Get-rich-quick Scheme
- When products to be shipped are not automated
- Payment option presented for business transactions are unrealistic and inconvenient for you.

Ways of avoiding fraud

When doing business online or investing in online business, you can avoid pitfalls and traps if you follow these steps.

a.   Learn to recognize red flags such as scanty information, unsolicited Phone calls or emails.

b.   Protect your personal information in your wallet and in your home.

c.   Don't give out your information easily. Know the person you are dealing with when giving out your information.

d.   Develop yourself to understand persuasion tactics of fraudsters.

e.   Always avoid wiring money for transactions.

f.   Make sure you check, ask and confirm transactions before investing in them.

3 CHAPTER THREE

How to set up profitable goals

Setting up effective achievable goals is what every business man needs to get results. Goals are the leverage we need in business to keep going forward with expectations of seeing success.

Setting goals follow different processes and each can be successful whether it's short term or long term goal. By failing to prepare, you're preparing to fail. Good planning is one of the keys to setting lasting goals.

Tools for effective goal setting

You can easily give up setting up goals when your efforts yield no results. Set goals and break them into tiny milestones. This is what you need to do everyday to get closer to your ultimate goal. When you have set up goals carrying out daily tasks becomes easier and lighter bringing motivation and focus keep you pushing forward.

1. Set goals your mind can visualize because what your mind sees is achievable. Write down your visualize goals on a paper. Example, you can write the amount you expect to get in your business weekly or monthly.

How are you going to achieve this, take time to describe in details meticulously as you can, knowing that you are likely to achieve your business goals.

2. Set achievable goals and believe in yourself wholeheartedly to see your goals manifest.

3. Be time focused – Have a launch date for your business and meet up that date if you want to achieve your goals.

4. Write down strong reasons you want to achieve the business goals.

5. Create milestones quarterly, weekly and daily goals to meet up your desired cash expectations. This will guide you in the right direction pushing you to achieve your business goals in the long run.

Planning is the key

Planning means being realistic about what it means to run a business. To be successful, think about the end result and how to achieve it. Create an action plan to follow that you are positive will give you the desirable results.

Don't just follow others; create a business you are passionate about. Create a vision for the future and develop strategic plans.

Tips on planning your business well

1. Develop a workable strategy for new product creation or quality service delivery to your targeted audience.

2. Plan for growth by setting targets and datelines.

3. Create room for innovations. You need to upgrade, update and renovate your plans if you want to be relevant in your business world.

4. Be familiar with all aspect of the market so that the target market can be defined.

5. Your business branding is also important by knowing what you intend to market and sell.

6. Have marketing and sales strategies – marketing creates customers and sales are generated by customers. Define your marketing strategies and channels to create your success.

Your motivation to succeed is the only thing that will enable you stay focus in the midst of hard times and challenges. Passion and commitment get your business going to the other side.

Steps to effective planning

1. Start asking questions about the business you are interested in doing. Make sure you have carried out enough research to know about the business background, promotion and know-how producing products, building a customer base and living out your vision in business.

Get connected to people of similar business, and learn from them for they all started like you.

2. Go ahead and start your business if you can overcome obstacles and get along till you arrive at your goals. It's your drive that will keep you motivated and overcome fear and failure.

3. Surround yourself with people of like vision. Forums and websites focusing on your business are places you can learn a lot from in your quest for expansion and results.

Let your focus be on your goals

It is true that many people struggle to meet their goals even when their expectations were realistic at the beginning. Life can get in the way when you are ready to take the necessary actions and make those vital changes makes you lose momentum and fail to focus on your goals.

This is where you blame everything for frustrating your efforts. The following tips if applied properly will help you reach your goals:

1. **Narrow your list** – Not too many set priorities. Take one thing at a time.

2. **Break major goals into smaller achievable plans** because large goals are overwhelming. Major goals can make you lose confidence and motivation thereby you should follow one step at a time and move on the next when that has been done.

3. **Tell people you trust about your goals** to make yourself accountable. Their support and advice will help you to stay focused.

4. **Record and measure your process** to know if you are improving or losing. Keep a record of achievement which you prepare weekly to provide an excellent feedback on your progress.

With hard work and consistent efforts, you can achieve your major goals in life in no time. Making $1000 monthly is feasible if you stay focused. Majority of people fail to meet up their expectations in business due to lack of required knowledge and skills.

It's easy to lose confidence if you fail to stay focused on your goals, but energized when you are focused.

Be accountable to yourself

For your business to succeed you must have the right mindset. Answering these questions will help you account for your business.

Why must I accomplish this goal?

How will it improve my life?

Nobody wants to sacrifice for something that's not worth it. **Read books and research people on your business, know what they do, how they breathe and all they do about their businesses to make it stand out.**

Learn from their interviews and pod casts, webinars, videos and everything you know they do and follow same to stand out. Making $1000 monthly is possible and feasible if you are ready to work hard until you see meaningful results.

Make it a priority to plan your schedule and block out those things that will affect your focus. Make sure your goal fit into your other schedules.

Develop yourself and acquire more information by researching, studying and reading more about your product and services. Knowing more about your business will strengthen you drive. See to it that every day you are working towards achieving your goals.

Patience – the key to lasting success

For you to last in business and get the desired results you need to exhibit patient. No long standing business ever strives on hasty and quick practices. To be successful, patience is needed in building up a brand, developing the brand and nurturing it to grow.

Furthermore, you need patience to communicate with your customers even when they don't trust you. There are some customers that will ask questions and make series of enquiries convincing you they want to buy but at the long run, they just fizzle out. In such a situation, you need patience to prevail.

Tips on using patience for business growth

1. With patience, you are bound to produce smart decisions after taking time to ponder and deliberate on issues of your business. These decisions definitely project you and sharpen your business plans in outsmarting your competitors.

2. Patience is a character that makes a business man excel and get outstanding results in his area of focus. The business can only move in the right direction if you have patience to monitor and try out new ways of doing business.

3. You can only master skills which lead to success if you have patience. Your reputation can't be dented when you stay off negative stories about success and focus on ways of becoming the best in your field of endeavor.

4. There is a proverbs which says "Slow and steady wins the race," meaning with patience you can work assiduously and steadily towards your goals and when you have reached your goals, you build a long standing reputation.

4 CHAPTER FOUR

Internet marketing principles

It is worthy of note that thousands of people start an online business every day. Out of these, only a minimal number succeed. The rest are either tired or can't meet up with other competitors. The reason why the rest of them failed is always attributed to mis-information; mismanagement and negligence of applying proven strategies known in aiding online businesses' growth.

Internet millionaires and other successful online marketers use proven strategies that still earn them income no matter the changes, or competitors in the market. These strategies are the basis of any online business. Therefore, for you to succeed, you must play by the rules to bring your online business to lime light.

These rules are so plain and simple that if applied with utmost discipline, and harnessing the power of the internet will project your business and keep it on track for years to come.

I will vividly explain with concise points each of these strategies which has helped many internet marketers including myself to overcome setbacks and get our businesses going against all odds.

Well defined workflow

In an online business, how you spend your time and plan your day matters. So it is imperative for you to set up your progression of tasks, events and interactions in order.

These can be achievable if you are determined to succeed by sticking to the following rules:

- Spend some time to create a comfortable workspace.
- Sort out your calendar and daily routine.
- Discuss and analyze your business processes.
- Document your processes.
- Look for ways to improve your business.
- Develop an outline on how your information should be stored.
- Highlight the areas that need improvement
- Put into practice your concepts and plans
- Set a day aside for administrative tasks.

Know your target audience/clients

Before you venture into online business, you must have a target audience you want to sell your products and services to. For you to reach your audience and get strangers which will eventually become acquaintances and in the long run your friends, you must do a bit of networking.

Networking involves advertising your products, introducing yourself to the people. Even if you are new with this, you need to learn to familiarize yourself with networking methods that may appeal to you. The methods are but are not limited to social media, emails, forums, blog sites etc.

Money management tips

Money management is a crucial aspect of business success both online and offline. If no proper money management skills, internet millionaires would have become broke in no time. Having your own money management skills and utilizing it effectively in your business, you will never be at loss in defining profitable channels.

This is when planning comes in. Planning is a vital key to money management. Planning requires that you have a budget, stick to it and manage the available resources you have to meet your needs today and in the future. It is planning that will give you confidence to execute and run your business without doubt or fear of failure.

I want to quickly show you some of the money management secrets used by internet gurus, millionaires and successful men that exist today both online and offline. You can carry out more research on the following information which will aid you in your business dealings.

- Don't invest more than you can afford to lose. Never be tempted above the amount you have set aside to invest.
- Take risk at times to succeed. There are some businesses that look risky to invest. But with foresight and common sense, you can take a bold step and come out smoking with profits.

- Always analyze your daily, weekly and monthly cash flow. Taking notes of increments and reductions.
- Develop a habit of saving money as if tomorrow will never come.
- Create a spending plan. Make sure you have a budget, follow your budget and no matter what, stick to your budget.
- Plan and set aside emergency funds. Who knows when the rainy day will come?

Record keeping that works

With so many work and innovations, you will discover that you have lost track of time and resources especially when your online business is booming and there is so much work to do. You will find it hard at this stage to stay up to date with internet trends, and at the same time continue to improve your business.

Sometimes, locating a client's information becomes difficult and you can't recall where so and so documents were kept. When this happens, you become agitated and find yourself under pressure which may cause colossus damage in the business you have taken years to build.

In any business I do, I try as much as possible to keep records of these items which I believe will guide you too to succeed.
There are but not limited to the following:

1) Ideas
2) Finances
3) Business transactions
4) Clients' details
5) Posts

6)   Invoices

A life away from home

It is paramount that you take some time off your business to cool off. This is because stress, pressure and tiredness can affect you physically, mentally, and psychologically. Therefore, get your brain refreshed always. Exercise to keep your senses alert at all times. Read inspiring articles when you are down.

Don't fail to spend time with your family. Play with them. Enjoy your life and have fun. Have a hobby you indulge in from time to time. By doing these things you will always find yourself awakened with new ideas and strength in to run your online business.

Not only that, you will be able to focus your attention on things that matters. And most importantly, you will always find challenges and setbacks interesting for in every challenge, there is an open door of opportunities.

Don't give up. Persist to Conquer

Keep trying new ideas and work harder even if there are no tangible results to show. Don't give up. Create new tactics and strategies. Put your brain to work. Review new techniques and re-invent your business ideas.

Learn to outsmart your competitors. Improve upon your quality and standard. Set a target and make sure you hit that mark, even if it is not your expectation. I know, it won't be easy at first but with persistency, consistency and determination, there is no barrier that can stand your exploits.

5 CHAPTER FIVE

Internet marketing game plan

When you are starting out a business online, the internet offers you nothing but options. But with a workable game plan, you will know which strategy is appropriate for your business.

And to survive in today's business world which is highly competitive, it is pertinent you take note of these important aspects which will help your business grow.

It is obvious that to live a life of continuous success in your business, you must be able to cater for the needs of your targeted audience.

Knowing what you want to achieve and how to know when you have achieved it.

To making $1000 monthly, your game plan should include and answer the following:

1. How you will promote your business/product?

2. Do you need to build brand awareness?

3. Will I drive traffic to the site or my audience?

4. Who will be my target audience?

5. Know the type of content your audience need.

6. How often should you connect with your audience?

When starting out in business, make yourself relevant but pace yourself and work according to how much you can do in the long run. Don't burn out yourself at the start and later have nothing to post.

How to connect with your customers

Every customer feels great when his queries are being answered. As a business man, you need to interact with your customers on a regular basis responding to their questions and queries.

1. Develop a plan that clearly communicates your goals and work towards a common purpose.

2. Determine a winning "strategy" that is focused on hitting your targets. Make sure your desired goals are clear and attainable.

3. Because challenges are inevitable, you must be ready to accept unanticipated obstacles that could truncate your plans.

4. Have a plan that you can efficiently, effectively get into action and not just the talking and planning.

Have a comprehensive offline marketing strategy. The strategy should be search engine optimization, google pay-per-click campaigns, email marketing, web designing, writing on blogs or social media tools.

Pick a niche to make money

For ultimate results, you need to pick a niche you are competent with that has a high volume of audiences, searches in search engines up to 1000 monthly searches and above if you expecting better results in return.

For this, you need to make sure you have knowledge of the niche and not just something profitable. You need to choose a niche depending on your ability. That is, anything for your expertise area.

If selling products that deal on money making ideas is what your targeted audience want, go for it, but please don't go into it because others are making tons of money on that. Be sure you have an expertise in that field. It is better you stick to weight loss products if you are conversant with weight loss and that's where your passion is.

Create your products around what you are knowledgeable about and you can easily write out articles surrounding that niche without problems. By doing this, you won't get bored at the long run if your passion is there.

Most people realize they ventured into something not in their field or expertise and fail woefully at the long run. That is the reason why thousands upon thousands of blogs and businesses are opened online every day and before you call out "JACK," there are no where to be found. If you don't have a passion in what you are doing, there will be no drive to prevail or continue when obstacles manifest.

3 keys to picking a niche

1. Pick on something you feel like doing and can unfold and express your thoughts and ideas through it. That is, something you have a passion for and can easily relates its benefits to others naturally.

2. Pick something that you can use your natural talents to refine the areas you'll like to grow.

3. See how it will inspire and help others. Look at it from a buyer's view and explain vividly the product or service you offer. This can bring excitement to guide you through the creation and packing of your product. A sure way you can make $1000 monthly.

Don't just pick a niche because you want to be profitable in it. Make sure the niche is what your audience need and can create a solution to meet their needs.

Remember, a niche is a problem your audience needs to be solved. Chose a niche that you know corresponds to your audience's needs. When you do this, a new world of options is opened up for you. You now understand where you can switch from someone struggling to find ideas for products to knowing instantly the type of products you should create and promote.

How to make easy money from your audience

1. Identify the problems your audience need is the key here. Carry out a research into the problems, challenges, aspirations and desires of your target audience. Get information about their problems questions people ask from forums, how-to websites and blogs.

2. Pick on the most profitable problems using monthly searches ratio picked from search engines related to the problems and stability of search terms related to the problems.

3. Know your competitors by using SEMRUSH to know what is trending and what people are interested in.

4. Keyword research is very important. Use keywords that are mostly search for and let your interest push you above and beyond your competitors.

33

Pick where you feel you mostly belong and serve them. If the place is right, making $1000 monthly will be the by-product of the great service you offered.

Find profitable market keywords for the niche, search for new niche ideas using Google keyword tool; it's absolutely free.

Pick keywords that pull in at least minimum 1000 global searches a month.

Niche picking tools

1. **Google Trends** – easily compare the world's interest in your chosen niche markets.

2. **Google Insights for search** - for search volume patterns across specific regions, time frame and categories.

3. **Magazines.com** – always list 10 top titles on their home page. These include fashion, entertainment, sports, finance, business, education, media, education etc.

4. **Ebay Pulse** – shows a daily snapshot of current trends and hot picks, listing popular searches and largest stores.

5. **Yahoo's Buzz** - showing hot events in entertainment industry.

6. **Amazon.com** – best site for market research showing top sellers, hot new releases, most gifted, shakers and movers of businesses.

7. **Google Adwords Keyword Tool** – gives you both keyword's and keyword phrase's search performance and it's seasonal trends..

8. **Word Tracker** – shows what people are really looking for online showing the exact keywords and phrases.

9. **Spyfu** – analyses your keyword letting you spy on the competition. It is free to use.

Steps to picking a working strategy

The internet has opened to us many opportunities of knowledge, inventing ideas and ways to develop ourselves, changing our orientations and providing a dozen other ways of improving connecting with others and making money.

As of today, many all over the world have been made to believe they can make money online as much as they want with a workable strategy. This clearly proves and shows to us that apart from the 9- 5 job, one can make it in life through the internet.

Making money online though possible is not as easy as posited. Most of the strategies flying up and down are just empty guides of get-rich-scheme which will make you go round in circles. Those guides are nothing but articles copied from the net and packaged into simple "Reports." After spending money on them you realize there is nothing special in them.

Does it really mean an individual can't make money online? No. You can make good money online but doing this does not happen overnight. To succeed online, you need a working strategy that has worked for others too.

If you want to make it on your own; it will require months of trials and error, couple with experiments to really know the right tools and strategy that will work. It takes more than just a strategy to make money online. The experts and marketing gurus will never want to reveal their strategies and they do so by selling such guides at a frightening amount which only a few could afford.

In this book, I will try as much as possible to highlight the ways you can know and pick on a working strategy to making money online.

5 principles prerequisite to making money online

Before we discuss the issue of strategy, let's quickly analyze the five principles that you must follow to make money online.

1. **Know your audience and know whom you are targeting**. The age, region, occupation, gender and marital status are the demographics you need to know about your customers if you really want to succeed in your online business.

Knowing these things will aid you to understand your audience and their needs.

2. **Add value to your brand.** Always add value to what you do and not rush after get-rich-quick scheme. When you give your audience value, your credibility is likely to increase. This doesn't happen overnight but takes time.

3. **Build trust with your customers.** Never convince people into buying something and later, they discover it was not worth it. When building an audience give them the room to trust you and believe in your products. By doing this they'll take your recommendations to heart.

They know that beyond the quest for profits you are providing value to them.

4.   Connect with your audience. To generate income online, you need to connect with your audience. This you do by letting them know more about your life. Be open and transparent with your audience providing them important information and lessons that you are sure they couldn't have had free of charge elsewhere.

Connect with them through posts, comments, and response you give to their questions, queries and most importantly, a sales funnel by having them on your list.

5.   **Collaborate with others in your niche.** You need to go out there and join groups, forums and blogs just to communicate with others in your niche. Be social and follow popular individuals in your niche, comment, share and like posts. Find like-minded individuals and link up with them engaging in conversation that will encourage exchange of ideas and tips.

Proven strategies for making money online

Two strategies are real and authentic to use online if you really want to make money online; that is, the long-term and short-term strategy. The long-term strategy opens up to a recurring passive income while on the hand; the short-term gives you quick cash.

The long-term strategy is the best strategy as you are sure getting recurring income in years to come. Also, sticking to its rules and principles, you can earn huge amount of income continuously. But this strategy takes time to yield results as well as painful when you work and doesn't see tangible results for some time.

The short-term though may give you fast results but the money doesn't last.

Different ways of making money from the strategies

1. **Build an informative blog** – Having a successful blog may be difficult at the start but it is the best way to make $1000 or above monthly if you are focused to make it work out as you desired.

2. **Sell services to customers** - Selling services is one of the ways you can make fast money online. Decide on the product to sell and work towards it.. Take your product to sites like Upwork, Fiverr, 99Designs etc and you'll certainly get results.

Note that it won't happen overnight but definitely, you'll make faster returns within months if not weeks.

3. **Sell products to your** audience – Think of the need of your audience and create a product to satisfy that need. It's the easiest way to get immediate relief to your financial woes.

Build an Amazon FBA business and you can setup an online store to sell your products. Use platforms like Esty, Shopify or E-junkie to do so. These platforms provide a quick-to-market solution.

4. **Develop Courses that sells.** This is one of the best income sources if you want to generate cash online. With a great online course, you are bound to making good amount of money monthly.

You can use platforms like Udemy or Skillshare to build and sell your courses.

5. **Provide Virtual Assistance.** You can make money by working for others using a specific skill you have. Writing articles for blogs, or doing

other things to virtually assist those in need, teaching musical instruments, tutoring for a language can fetch you good money.

6.　　**Writing of books.**　Books are what everybody need today for information and leisure.　Books are the best ways to convey your thoughts and experiences to help others who may find themselves in similar situations.

Write what people would like to read such as DIY tutorials, money making guides, self development tips, educational books, and religious books.　Use platforms such as Amazon KDP, Smashwords, Kobo, Payhip among other numerous sites to publish your books.

All these are the platforms you can leverage to make money online without leaving the comfort of your home.

6 CHAPTER SIX

Online platforms for creating websites

A platform is what lifts you up and on which others can stand. To make money online, you need to build a digital platform that you can easily connect with others, create products and give values.

Your platform should be able to attract audiences and customers. Your platform can be a website or a blog or an auto-responder domain, a place where you can connect and interact with your targeted audience.

Hottest platforms nowadays are Facebook, Instagram, Twitter and Youtubr. There are termed social media platforms for promoting photos, videos and words messages.

Popular DIY Platform Options

These are platforms you can build your site on their free or paid templates. These kinds of platforms are great for beginners but as your business grows, you migrate to something bigger and better.

1. **Squarespace.com**

One of the best one stop shops for creating beautiful sites and portfolios to ecommerce sites.

Features:

- ❖ Ease of user
- ❖ User interface is pretty
- ❖ Self explanatory and
- ❖ Easy to navigate
- ❖ Videos and articles in their Help section in case you are stuck

Price starts at $24/ month

2. Wix.com

This site gives you blank canvas editor where you can pick the features and layout of your website with just a few clicks.

There are impressive functionality especially for such a simple platform to create ecommerce shops and blogs. Wix platform is made for those with no idea of computer operations as they can drag, drop and create a wix website in no time.

Here the price is between $14 -$30 per month depending on what you choice.

3. Weebly.com

Weebly.com is free platform where you can drag and drop to your defined template with their website builder. Here you are allowed to build well-designed websites quickly.

Weebly.com has an "App Store" which helps you to quickly add new functions to your site.

4. Shopify.com

This is an ecommerce platform that allows you to set up and run an online shop from anywhere around the world without leaving your living room. If your desire is to make money online through an online shop, then you need to use this platform.

Hybrid Platforms

1. Wordpress.com

This is the most widely used platform in the world for building websites. It's an open source website creation tool with content management system feature. There's a lot you can do with wordpress. It has thousands of plug-ins that can do virtually everything from building a custom contact form to optimizing your website for search engines to automatic back up.

There are also thousands of responsive themes you can select from to give your site an inviting appearance.

Wordpress is said to be best platform for beginners, amateur and professionals who want to take their online business to another level.

Wordpress is free to use.

2. Jimbdo.com

A template based website builder that lets you build good looking responsive websites with no coding knowledge and skills necessary. Jimbdo,com supports any kind of business with features like ecommerce capabilities, portfolio options. It is great for beginners.

Editing and changing things like font and color is super simple. All features can be added to your site with just a few mouse clicks.

Choosing the best web platform for your business is most important, but you can't make the right choice if you don't know what you need.

Get clear on what you want from your website and then find the web platform that suits your needs.

Building a Brand that Stands Out

A brand makes you stand out from the rest and it's about all the experiences your customers and potential customers have with your business.

A strong brand portrays the business, its activities, its mission, and at the same time pursues trust and credibility.

Your brand grows through your daily interactions with customers, your response to their questions, the content of your posts on social media among other things.

Tips for Brand Development

1. **Always be unique** – Think differently and be known for what you stand for. Be known for something.

2. **Grow your audience** by providing services/products that add value and bring trust.

3. **Build great products and services.** Create promotional materials that identify your brand and suit your audience.

4. Be consistent. Don't relax in offering good information and tips about your products and services to your audience as this will create familiarity and ends in trust.

5. Keep your promises to your customers.

6. Stand for something

7. Make sure apart from profits you get from selling your products; always deliver value to your audience.

Have Your Own Email List

Email marketing is the best form of marketing so far if you desire to make good income online. It is still the smartest thing you can do and if done rightly, can continue to fetch you money online for years to come. Without an email list, you will struggle to make it online.

Why Email List is Important.

1. You can email more offers on a regular basis to your audience without any problem.

2. The conversion rate when it comes to sales is always high compare to other marketing platforms.

3. It engages your audience in a creative personalized way that get them hooked to your contents or product features.

4. An outlet to prove to your customers you know their problems and can provide solutions.

5. It is the simplest way to make sales with new customers and build deeper relationship with them. It is the joy of your audience to hear more from you than you realize.

6. Email offers protection providing you the only way to build a lasting relationship with your clients.

When you build an email list, automatically it is yours for keeps. No other person can change the rules for you.

With email list you can easily engage with your audience, drive new business, promote products and protect yourself from changes in Search Engine Optimization.

Start building an email list today.

Ways of making money with Email Marketing

1. **Building a membership site** is the legit way to profit as it stands to give you recurring income. To make more money online, put your efforts to creating channels that produce passive income.

With a membership site you can make up to $1000 to $5000 every month depending on the number of subscribers you have on your list.

To succeed in this, you need to offer great value which can't be access for free from elsewhere.

2. **Recommend Great Products/Services.** As a blogger, there are products and services you have been using that you can recommend to your email list. Creating a short video or tutorial of a product and send it to your list. Because of the level of trust they have in you, they will gladly buy the offer. If the product was an affiliate product you are such of making good commission from your list.

3. **If you are into promoting CPA offers** you are sure of gaining more money from your referrals. For example, a web hosting company looking for leads may pay you $10 – $20 per referral.

A simple survey you tweet or send to your list can generate over $1000 for you. This is a huge profit for doing nothing.

4. **You can develop a product or write an ebook** and then sell to your audience, that is, email list. You only need creativity to become a product owner.

If you can't put a book together, then you can hire or seek the help of a freelance writer for a fees.

5. **Give Out Free Premium Course.** You can definitely prove your worth by giving free premium course to your list. Be good at what you do and they will buy from you as long as they are on your list.

How to build a successful email list

A successful email list that makes money is a system created to bring results. For you to attain this feat, you must develop a strong relationship with your list members.

1. **Find a market that has a need** and understand what their need is.

2. **Understanding your market**, knowing what they want, how they spend and why they joined your list in the first place will help you in delivering effective content to them.

3. Have an incentive to make people join your list. You can create an ebook or write a free course in exchange for their emails. Let it be an incentive you are an expertise in or related to your blog, products or services.

4. **Give away a discount or a coupon**. Most online stores use this method to attract customers and get them on their list.

5. You can have a sign up form on your blog and offer an ebook or a free course or services in exchange for email.

Tips on having an email list

Firstly, give away tons of information and value for free and then start offering relevant products or services that will help them.

Secondly, you send an automated emails to your already subscribers follow up series to offer more free value to your list like 5 or six times without selling anything but just to build trust.
After getting trust, you start offering them products or services.

Make sure your offers are relevant to your audiences or subscribers base.
Once there is trust you stand a chance of making more money from them.

7 CHAPTER SEVEN

Focus on one ... not all.

There is no end to making money online. It's virtually easy when you are armed with a method or niche that you developed to sell online. Though making money online per say is not easy but with determination and focus plus an hour or two of work, you are in line to making a passive income online.

The internet is full of methods, techniques and ways of making money. From one website to the other including social media, you will be bombarded with different make money schemes and it left for you to make a choice out of the thousands and stick to one.

The following are the Fail-Safe Online Money Methods that are used by virtually all internet marketers over the world.

Fail-Safe Money Making Methods

Cost Per Action

CPA is one of the easiest businesses on the net that you do. CPA simply means Cost Per Action. As the name implies, it is a lead generating marketing program whereby a company pay you to generate lead (client).

There are over 100 CPA companies online. You just need to research for the best among them and select the one you'll be comfortable doing business with. Of the various CPA companies, maxbounty.com and affiliaxe.com are the most popular.

Affiliate Marketing

Affiliate marketing is when you earn a commission by promoting other people's products. You can do this by selecting a product you like, promoting it to other individuals and you earn a percentage of the profit if they buy the product.

There are two ways of approaching affiliate marketing;
- You can offer an affiliate program to others.
- You can sign up to be other business affiliate

Some of the best affiliate programs out of the tons of affiliate programs online to make money from are Amazon associates, Clickbank, Linkshare, Commission junction, Paydotcom, Vistaprint, ShareAshare etc.

Blogging

Blogging is a money-spinning online business. It is easy to set up and maintain blogs. Imagine a life where you are paid to write on things that interest you, whenever you want, wherever you are. The simplicity of blogging if understood can help you generate a passive online income.

There are several options of getting a blog. You can decide to host a blog on your own domain or get a free blog. For newbie, let's talk about the free blogs. You can obtain a free blog at www.blogger.com. You can also get a blog at www.wordpress.com. Wordpress is a free blog engine that is robust and noticeably expandable.

Blogger.com is owned by Google, blogger sites are quickly picked up by search engines and indexed faster. Wordpress.com, however, is widely used because of its multi-faceted features.

Article Writing

Writing articles to make money online is something that has been there since the inception of the internet and has continues to grow daily. Any product that must sell should have a solid content that is captivating, satisfying and interesting. Article Writing is the only way quality information is expressed and because of this, has become one of the hottest things on the internet. And it's true that articles are an awesome and easy way to make money online.

With articles, you sure can:

- Generate quality traffic to your website.

- Send traffic to your affiliate websites.

- Use several of them to quickly create your own e-books and sell them on mini sites and blogs.

Flipping of Websites

Flipping of websites is another way of making money online. You can either purchase a ready-made niche website or build one on your own. The easiest way is to buy someone else's website. Make sure the site you buy has SEO contents that can be captured and indexed easily by search engines. You can then go ahead and sell your finished website on www.flippa.com.

Joint Ventures

Some people on their own can't work effectively except they team up with others. When people come together to run a business, there is a synergy created that propel the business to grow and hence more profits.

Joint Venture is excellent for payment gateways, online merchants' sites etc. Last note; do not enter a Joint Venture unless you are ready to take a large responsibility.

Forex Trading

Forex as the name implies has to do with Foreign Exchange. Selling and buying of currencies online is carried out 24/7 from Sunday night till Friday night every week except on holidays.

Forex trading needs more of calculations; more studies and daily news follow up if you desire to succeed. Here charts plus technical analysis are the basis used for buying and selling foreign currencies for profit making.

Forex trading is a high risk investment that yields profitable returns. With determination, good training and a good strategy, you can overcome all odds and start making good money.
There are brokers all over the web and you can choose one if you are keen on this type of business.

Niche Marketing

Even though online market is large and businesses vary, to succeed; you must make a choice out of the numerous businesses. You need to, first of all, select a product to sell or promote. You then look for available resources on those products.

Look for resources that will help you to dominate niche market with these keys.

Find a specific market with specific need relating to your selected product.

Create products that address these needs.

Promote the products and start making money.

Lastly, for you to succeed online, you must HAVE a NICHE. For you to get desired result from your niche, you need to DEFINE your MARKET. With these tips in your mind, there is no end to your profitability.

CONCLUSION

I want to share with you some of the things I have learnt over the years while doing business online which I believe will aid you immensely in running your online business.

1. Educate yourself as often as possible

- Read wide.
- Attend for seminars and trainings.
- Educate yourself as often as you possibly can.
- Don't be outdated. Develop yourself by investing in online courses, buy manuals, read wide on internet marketing to be able to give something that has value.

2. Always be honest

If you lie, you will lose your credibility. Be disciplined and true to yourself in all honesty. Know that without credibility your business is as good as dead.

3. Be balanced

Don't be obsessed with doing business online. But be balanced and diversify your activities. So you'll be more productive with these.

4.   Promise more than your competitors and over-deliver

Make sure your offers are irresistible because there is too much competition online. Then make your customers happy by giving them more than what they want.

5. Diversify your activity and adapt to new

Diversify by investing in at least two businesses. Don't put all your eggs in one basket. Be opened to use new ways of making money online.
If you want to make money in life, seize every opportunity you have with both hands.

I hope you found this ebook useful. If you'd like to thank me or for further information, the nicest way would be to contact me through surfdealz@gmail.com

Thank you!

ABOUT THE AUTHOR

Bassey Jimmy is a businessman, writer, and an Internet marketing expert. He is the president of *Believe Marketing Inc.* and the author of many other books to list here, including *Top Proven Strategies For Making Money Today.*

He left banking nine years ago and since then has taken the internet by storm.

Mr. Jimmy is happily married to Esther and they have four lovely children.